Aa

a

[a]

Sounds like "a" in "father" or "after"

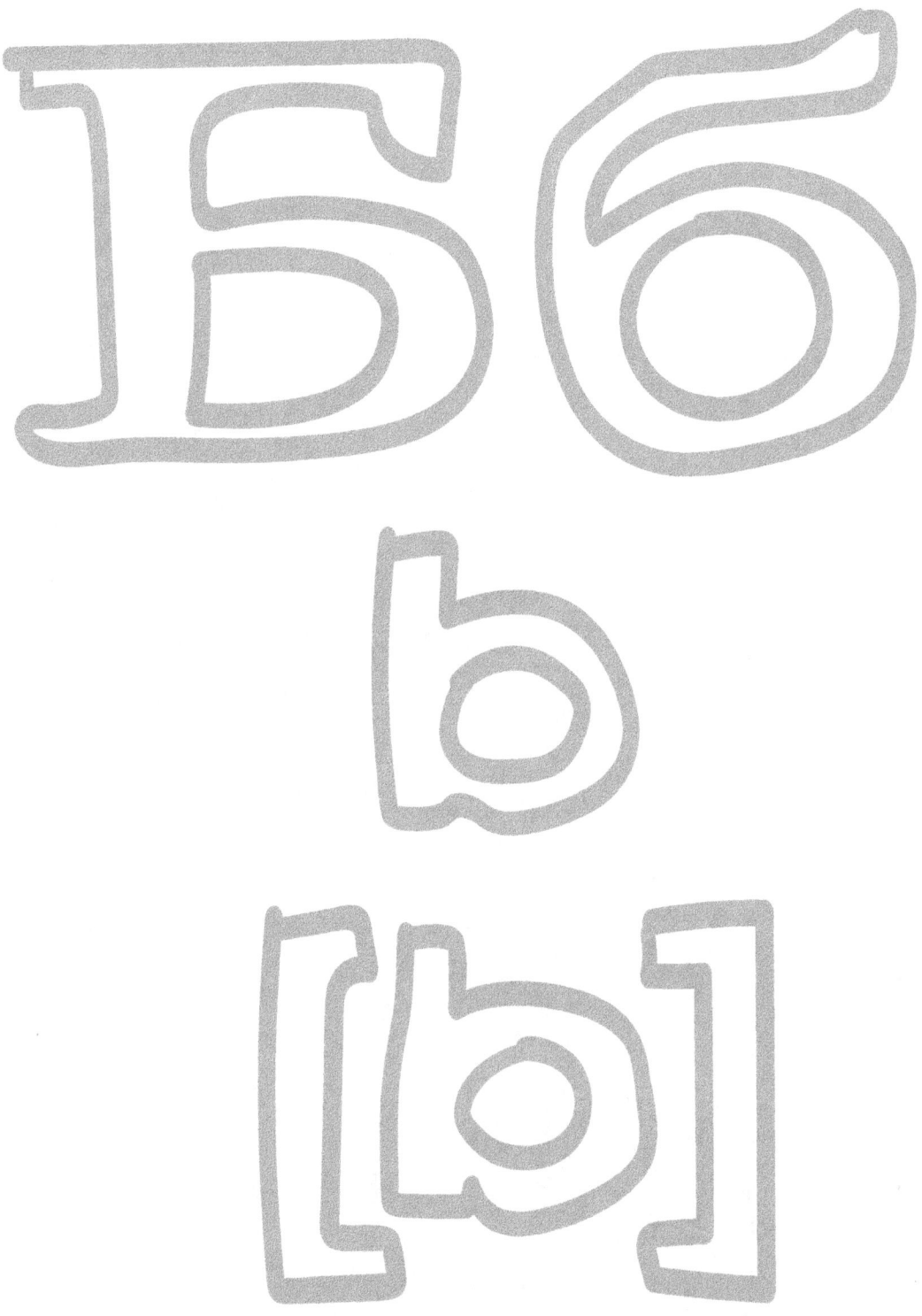

sounds like "b" in "bad" or "blue"

B b

v

[v]

Sounds like "v" in "van" or "voice"

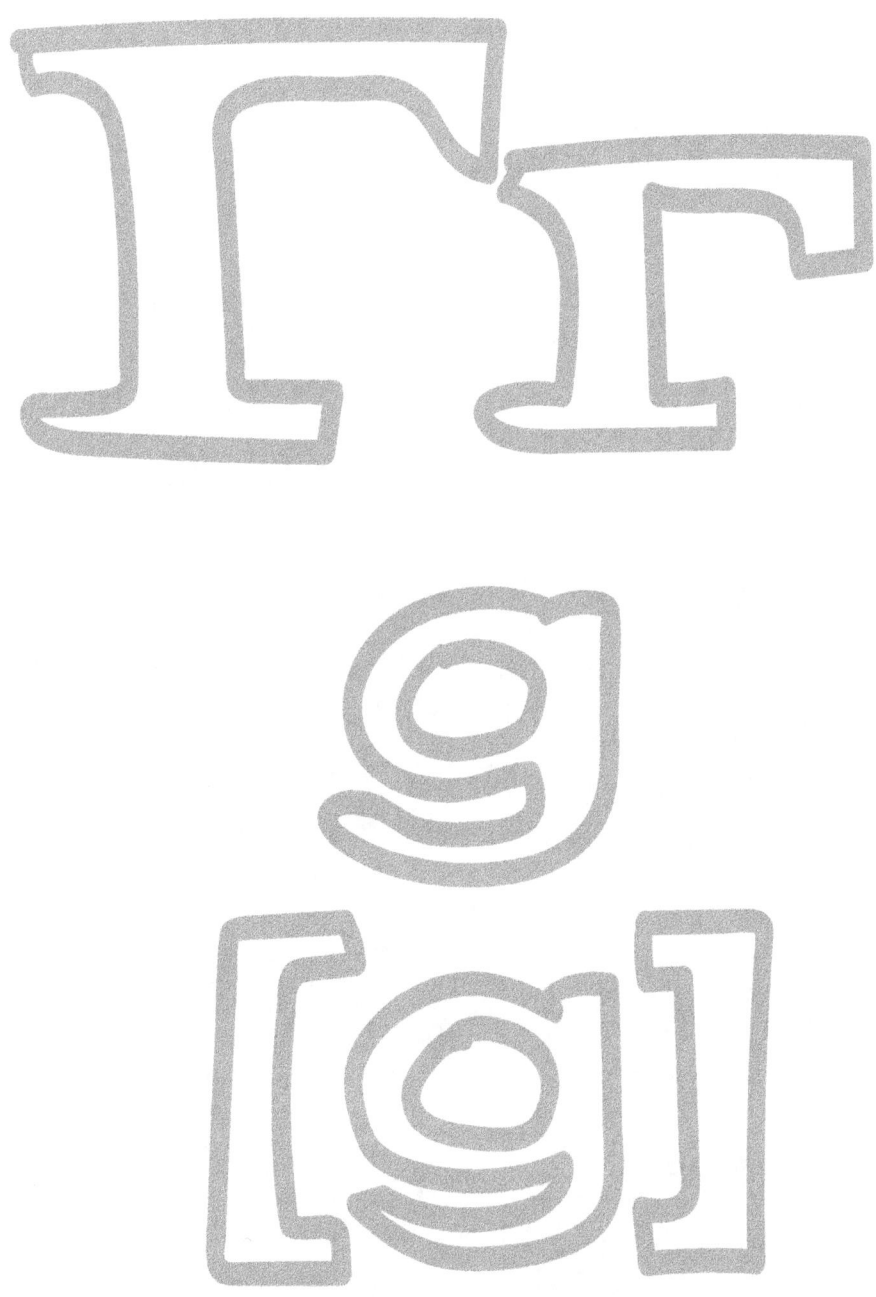

sounds like "g" in "go" or "guard"

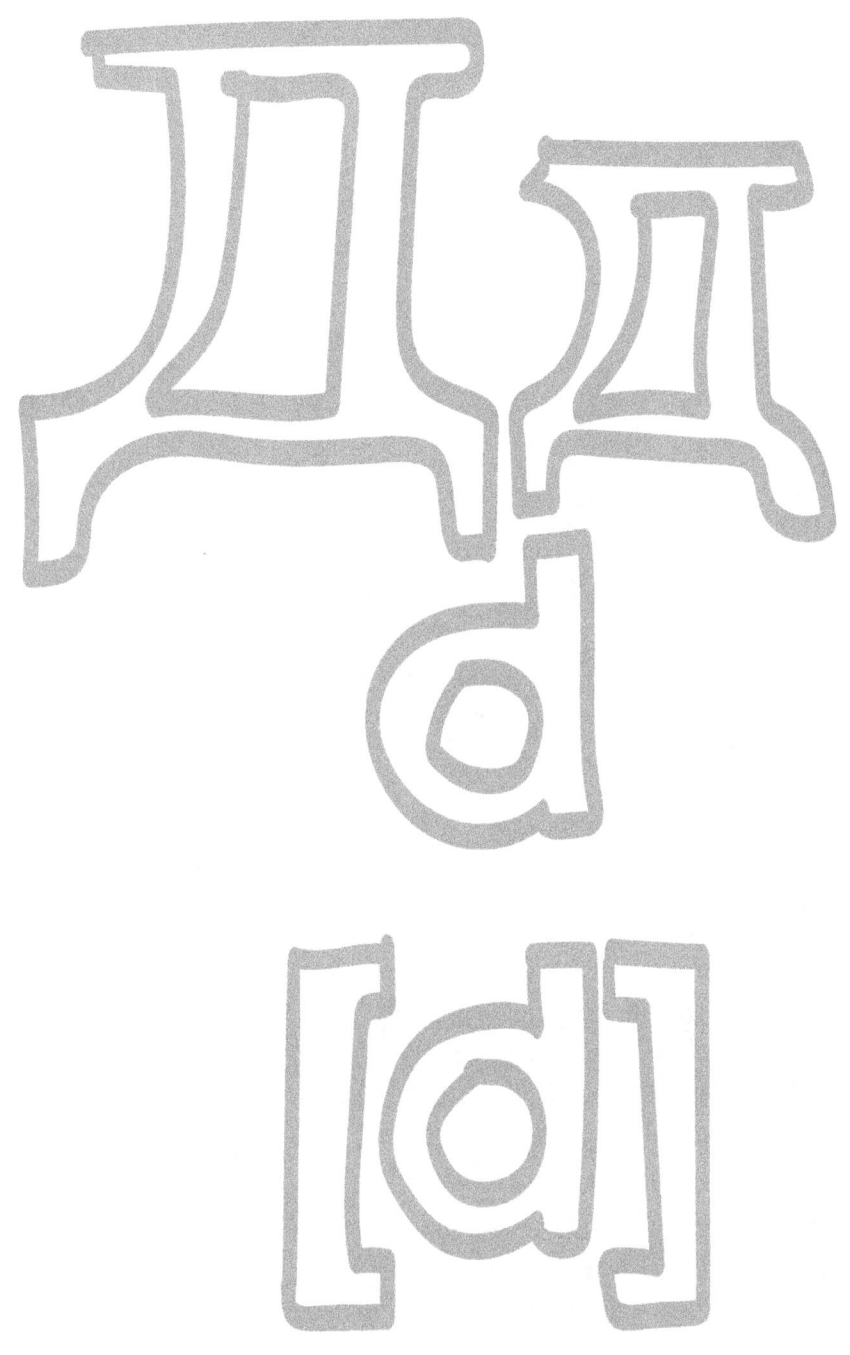

Sounds like "d" in "done" or "double"

sounds either like "ye" in "yes"

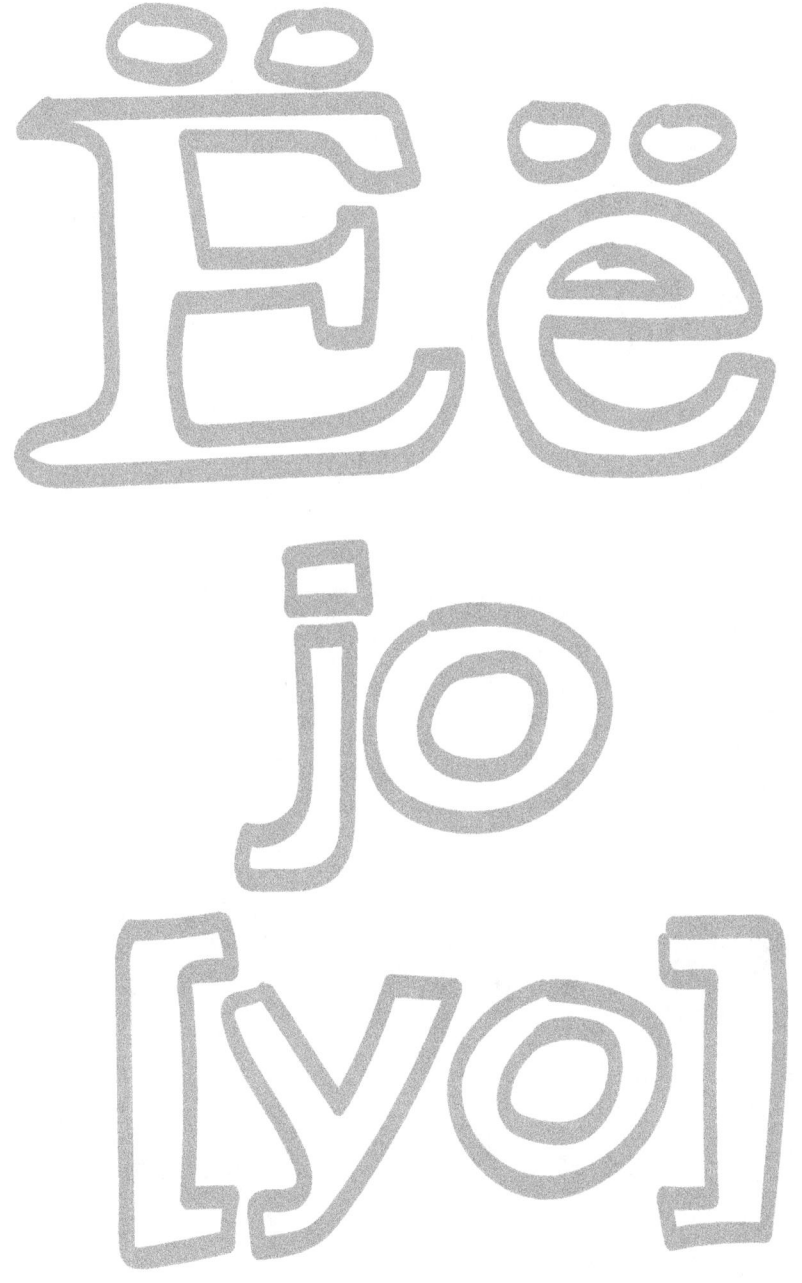

sounds like "yo" in "your"

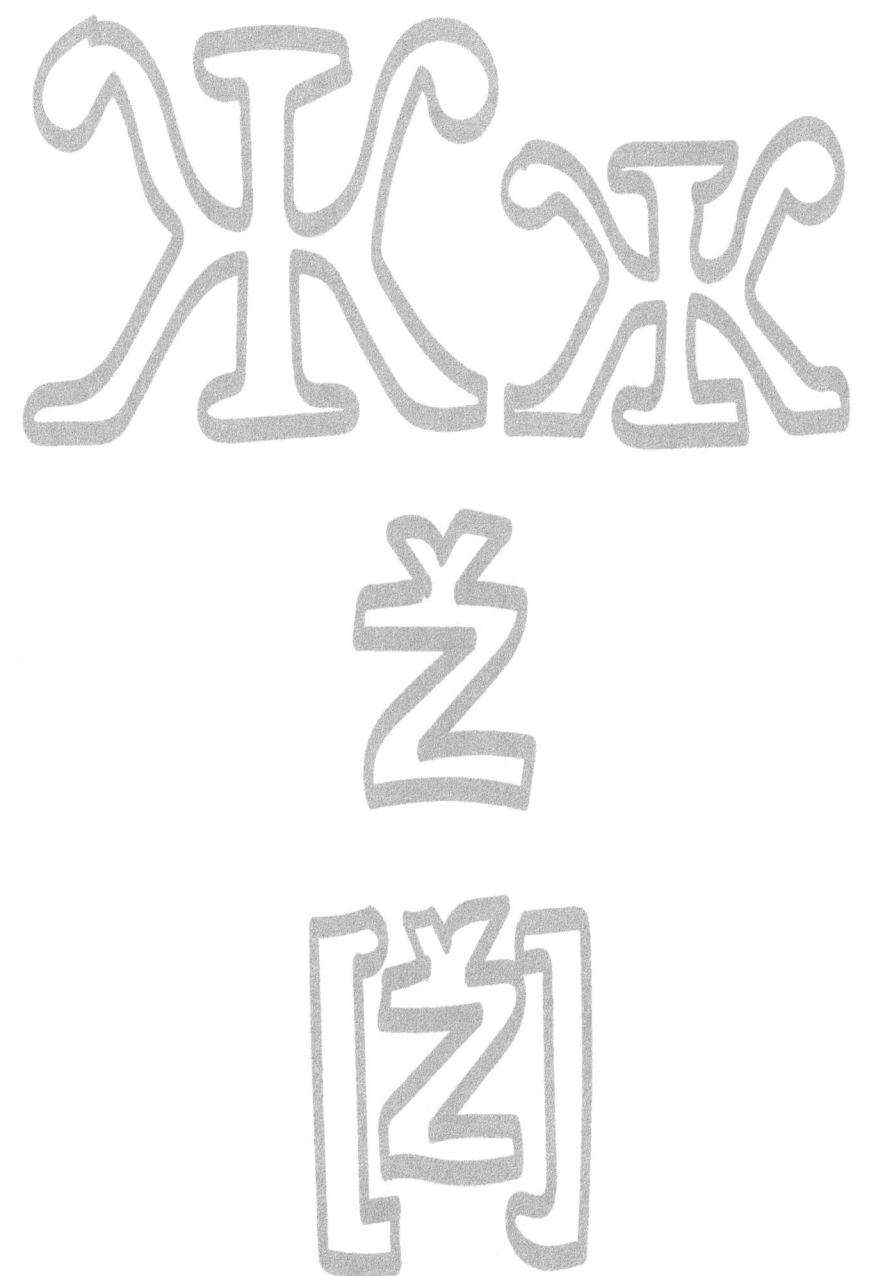

sounds like "s" in "usual", "pleasure", "measure" or "treasure"

"z" in "zoo" or "zodiac"

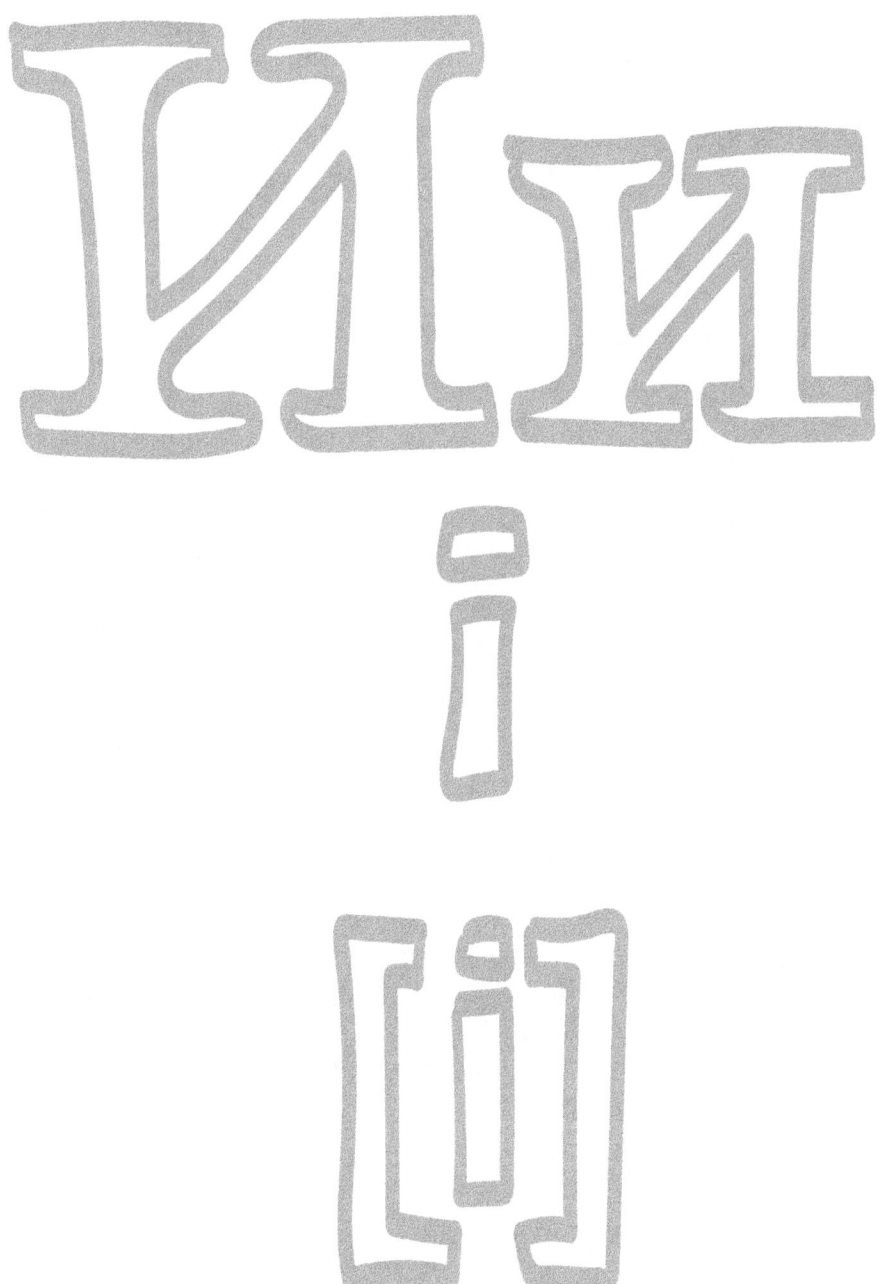

sounds like "ee" in "see", "free" or "meet"

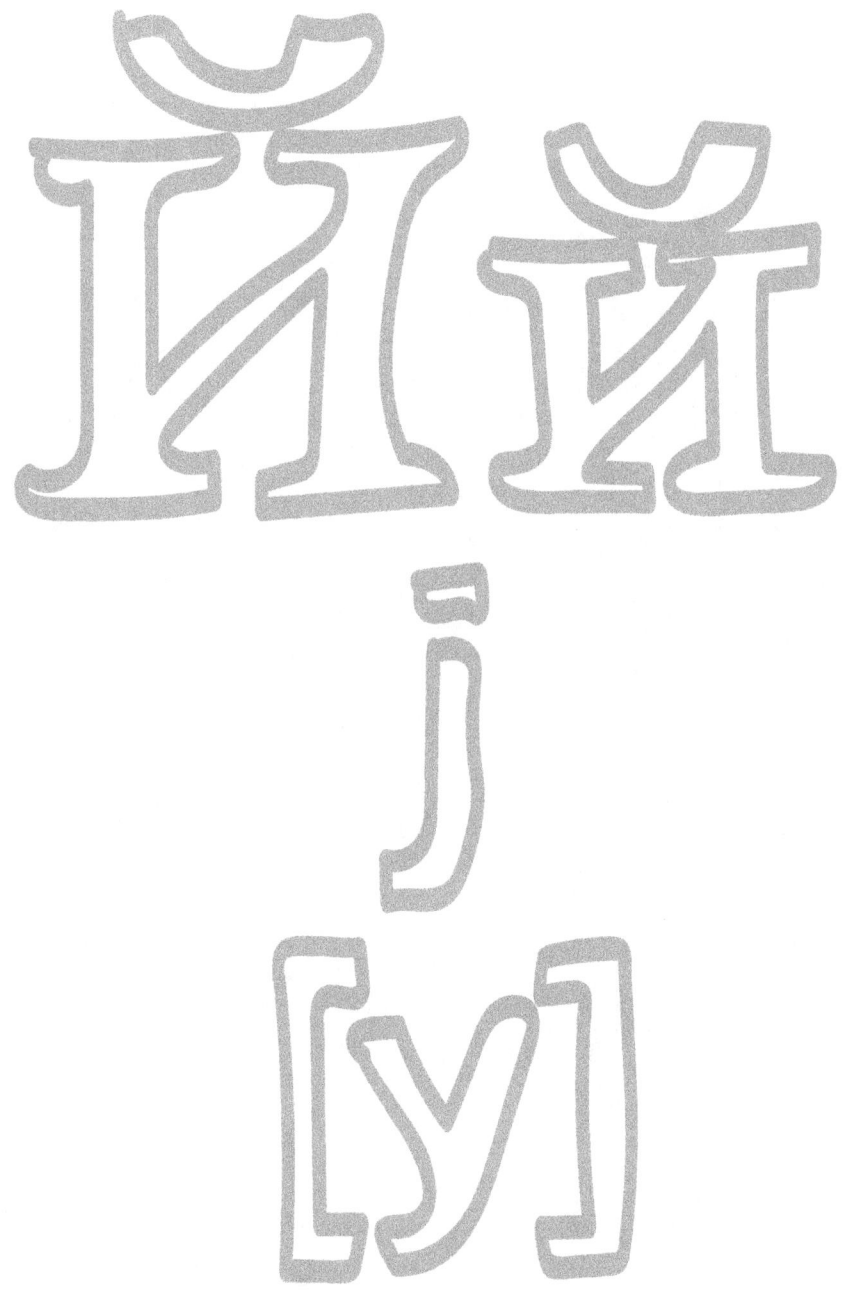

sounds like "y" in "toy" or "oyster"

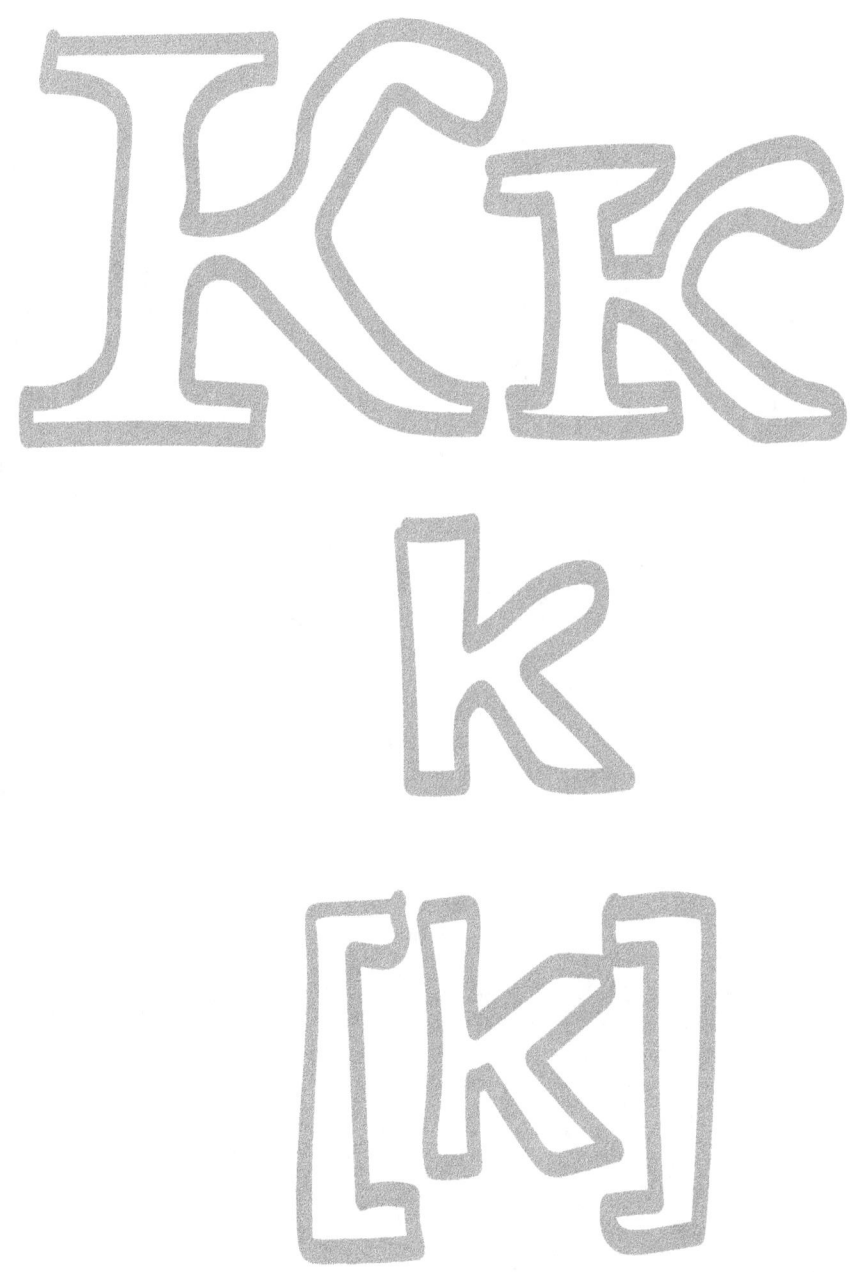

sounds like "k" in "kept", "kite" or "like"

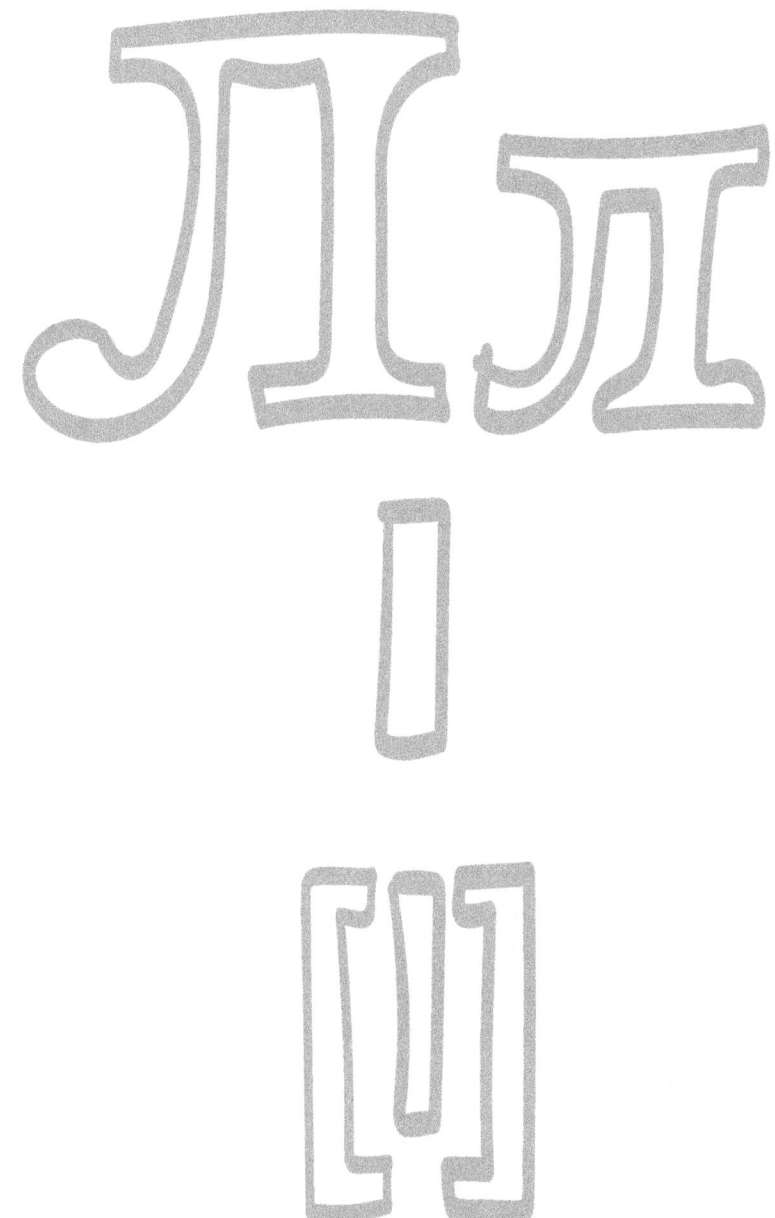

sounds like "l" in "lamp" or "chill"

sounds like "m" in "mother" or "mobile"

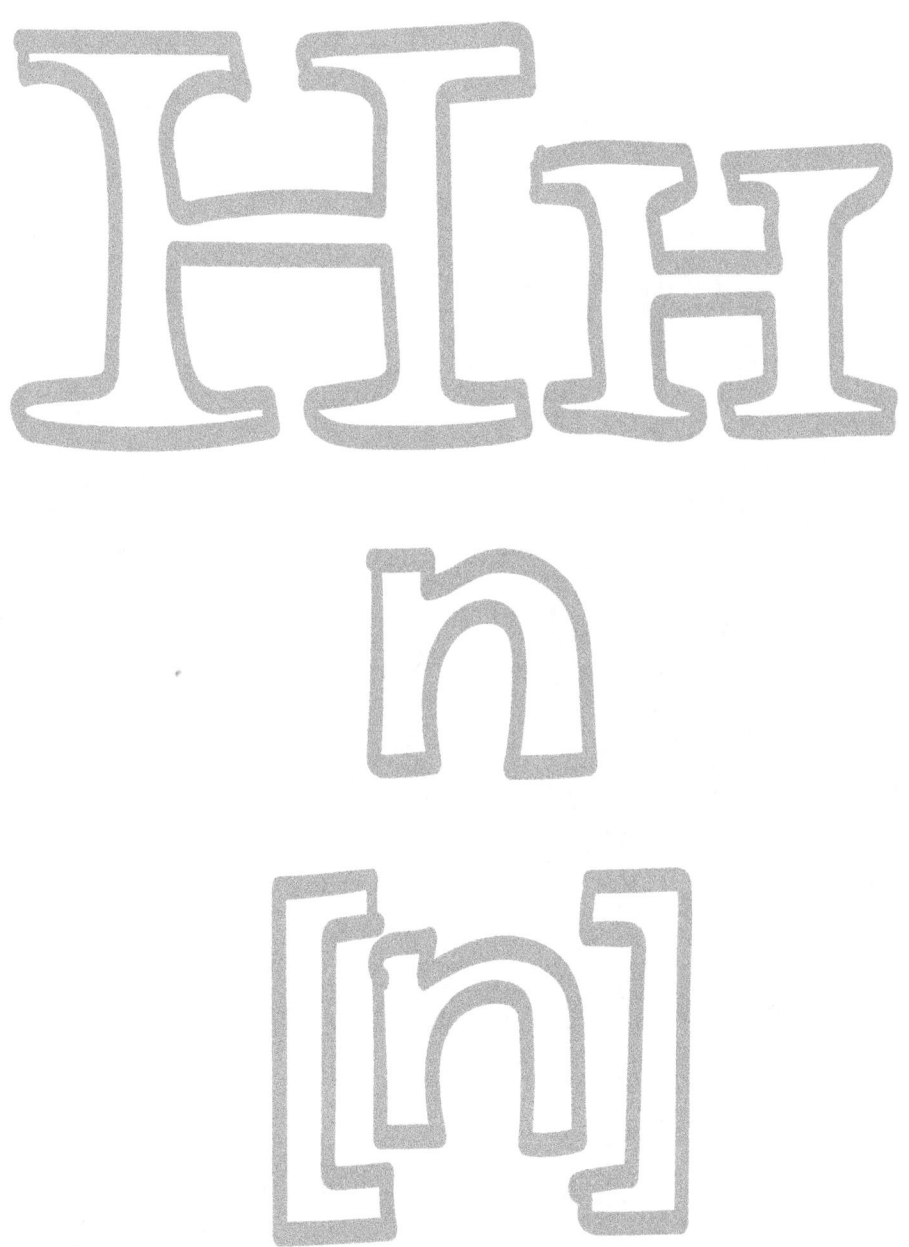

sounds like "n" in "no" or "noon"

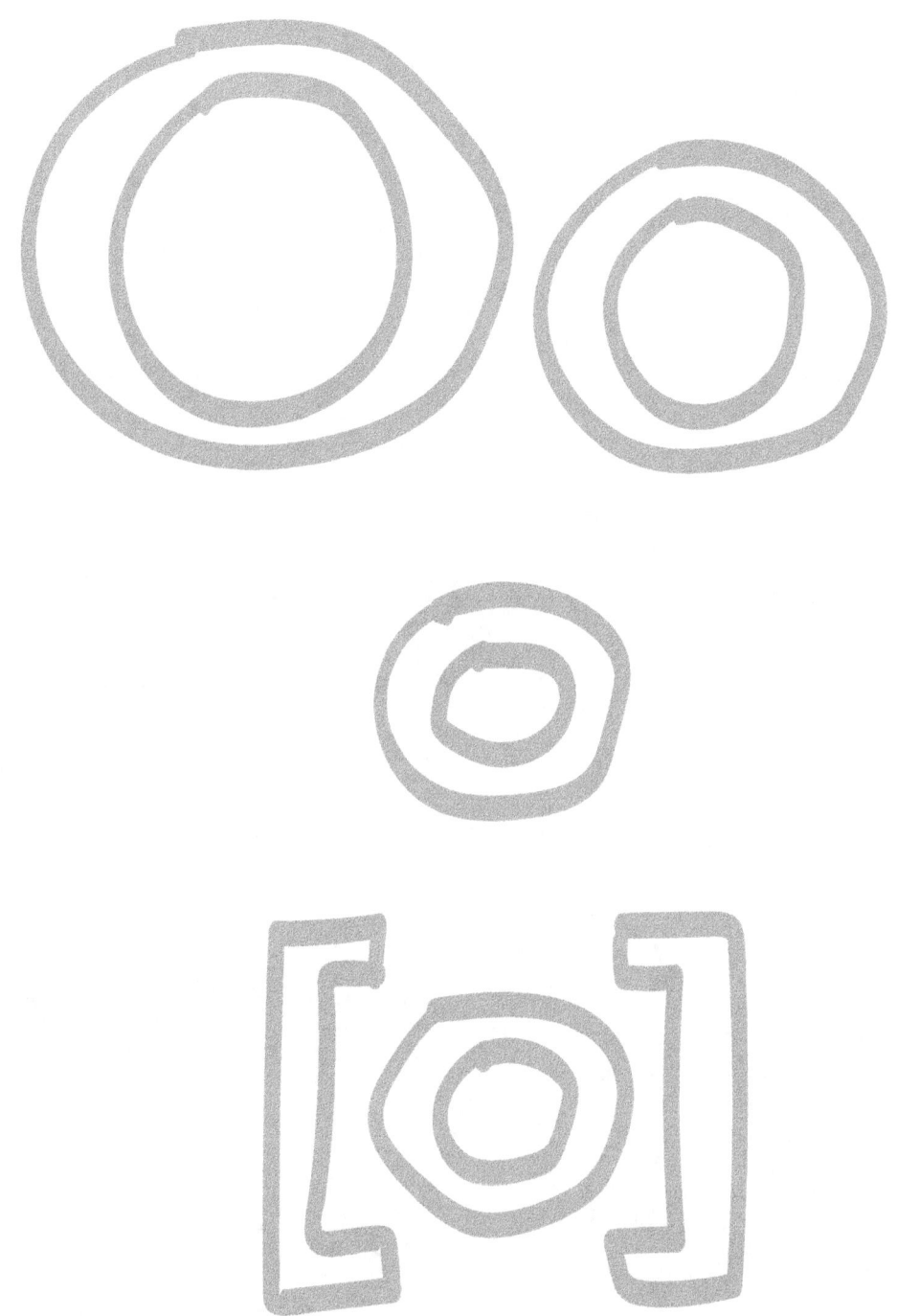

sounds like "o" in "bore" or "more" (without the 'r' sound)

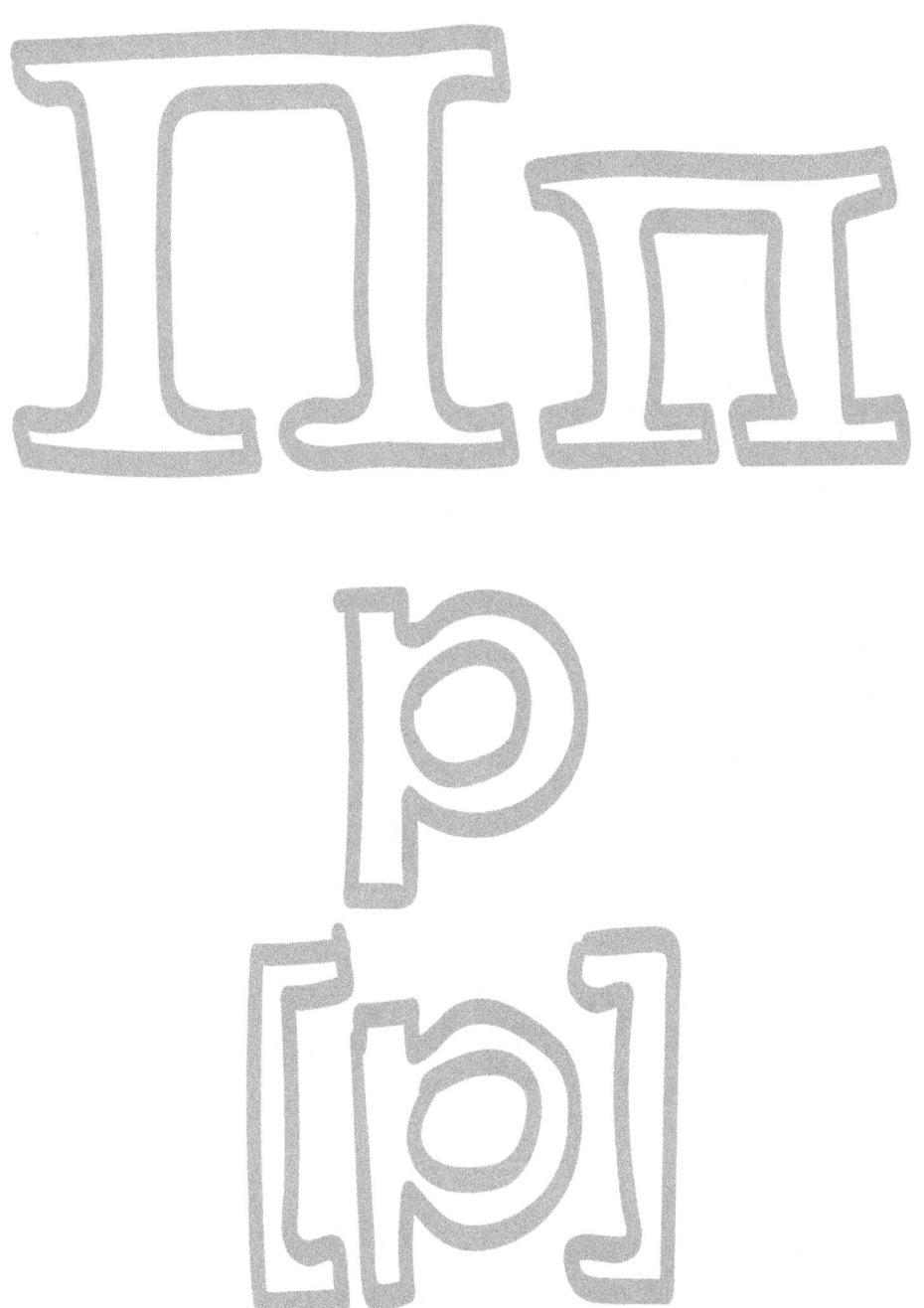

sounds like "p" in "potato" or "compassion"

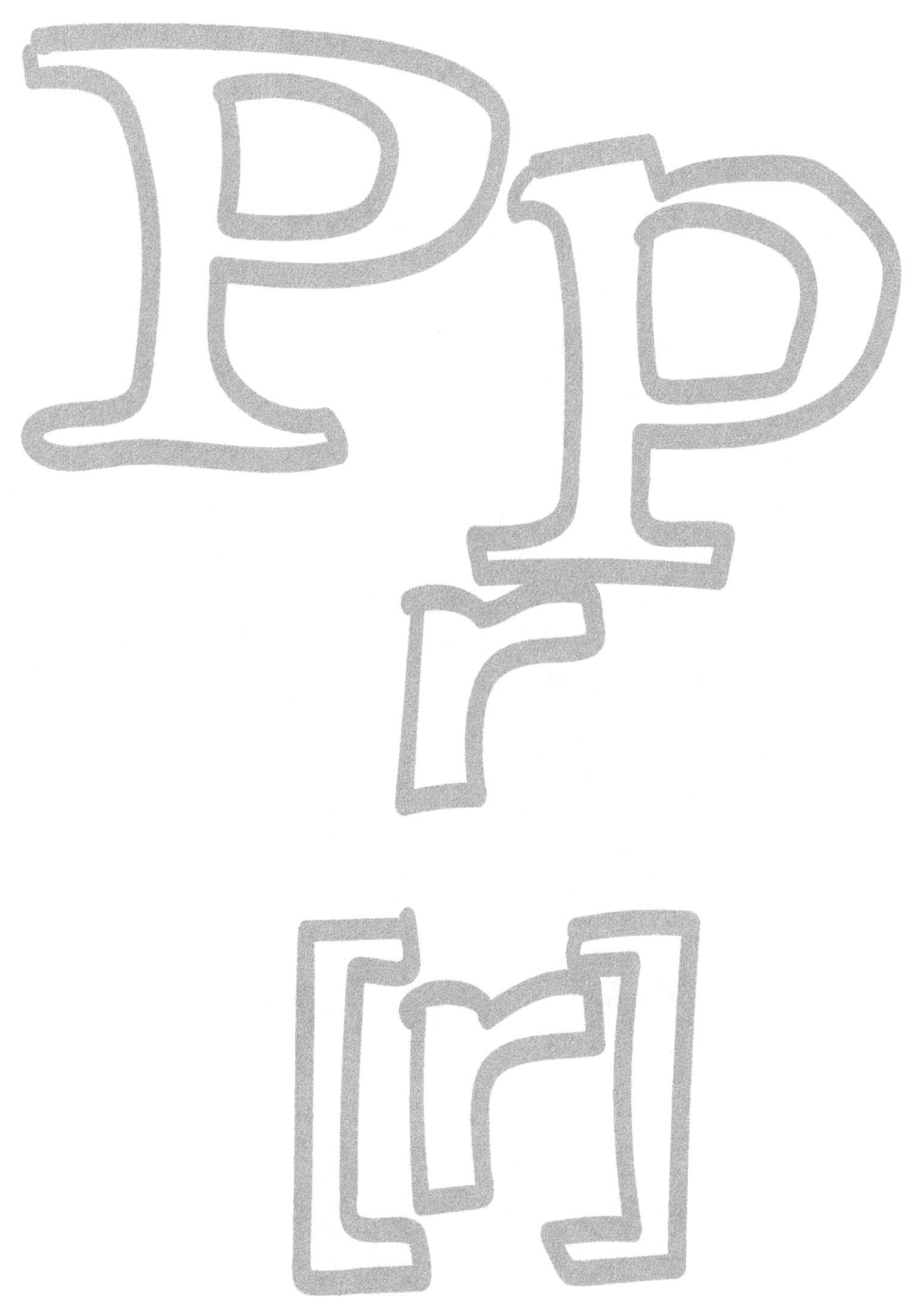

sounds like "r" in "run" or "rest"

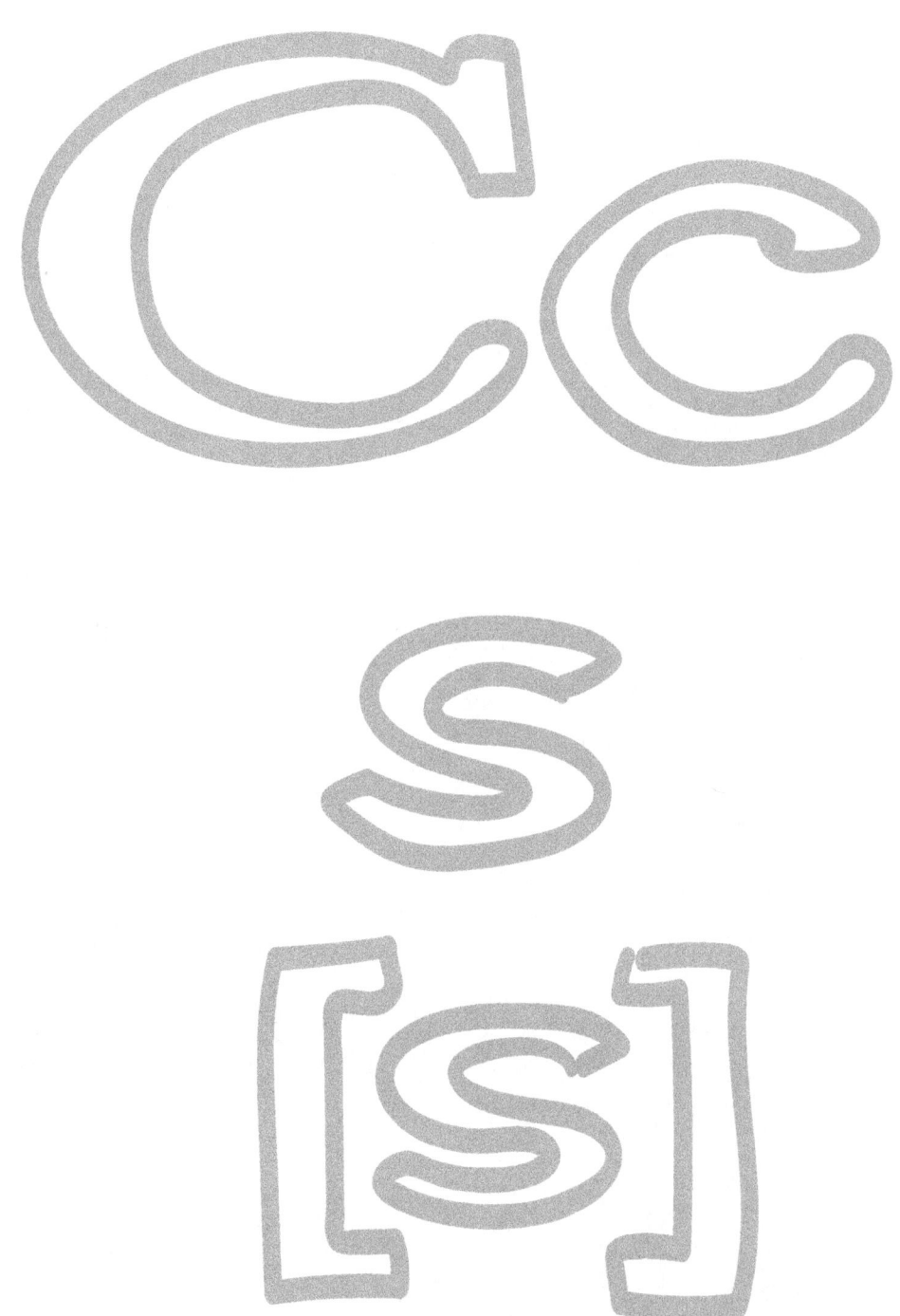

sounds like "s" in "stone" or "sale"

sounds like "t" in "top" or "task"

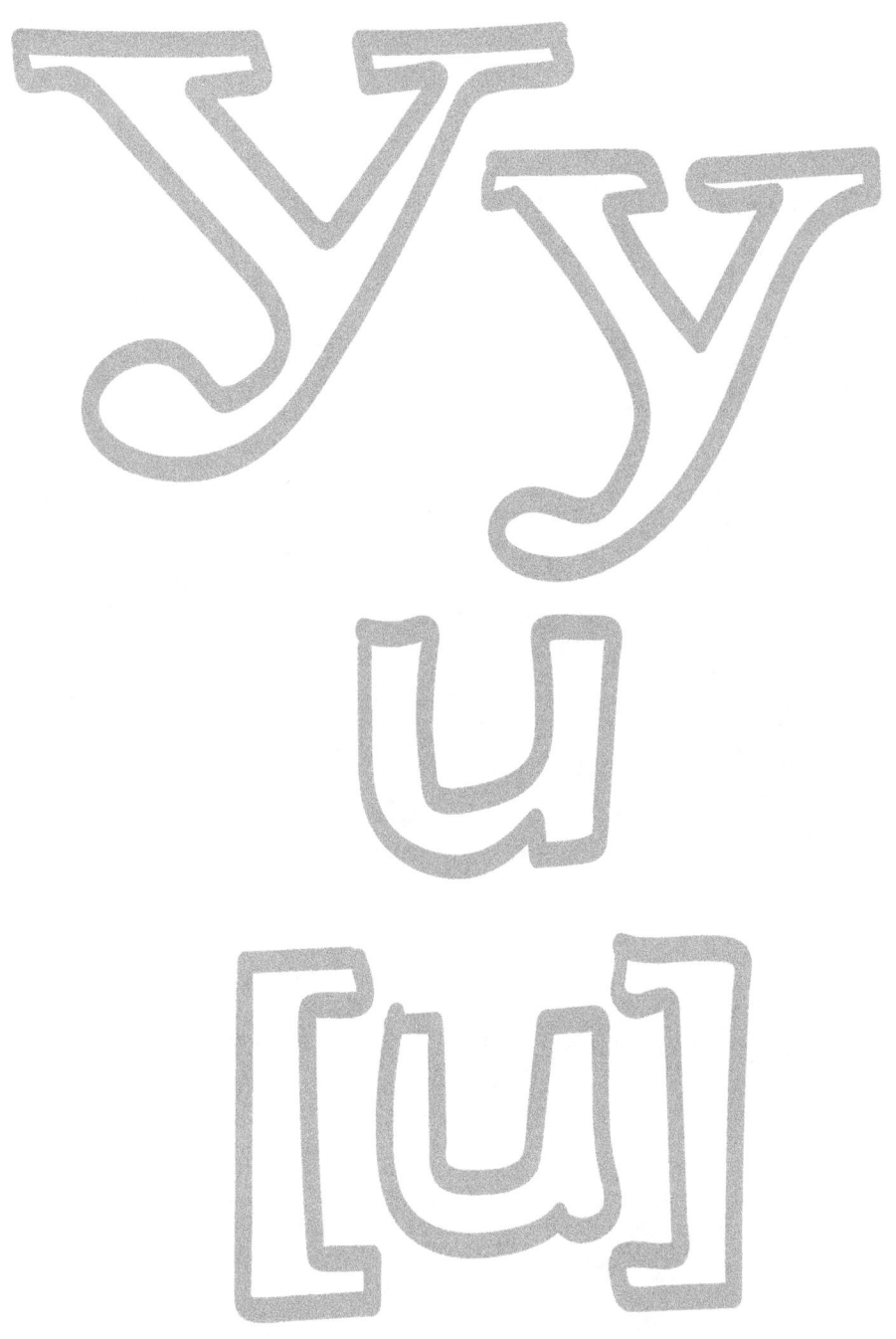

sounds like "oo" in "tool"

sounds like "f" in "face" or "fact"

sounds like "ch" in "loch"

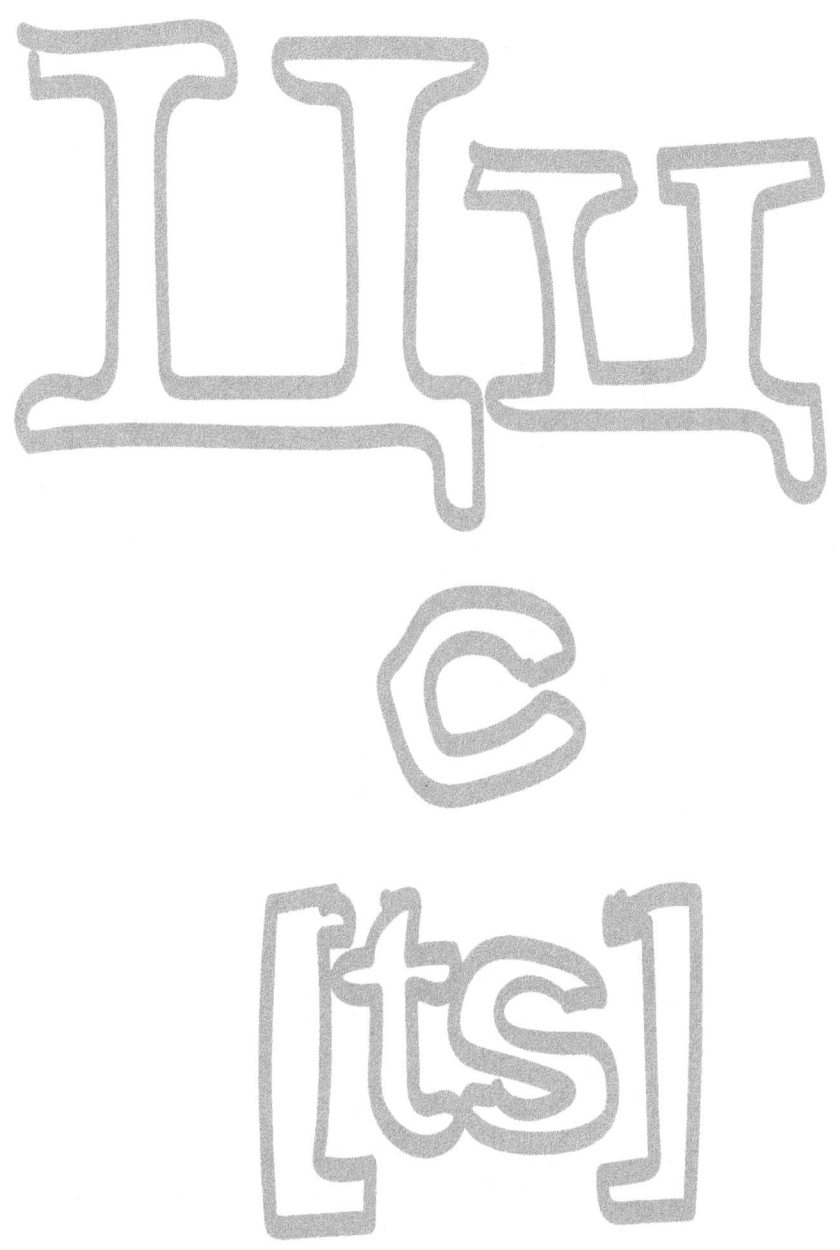

sounds like "ts" in "sits" or "that's"

sounds like "ch" in "chat" or "church"

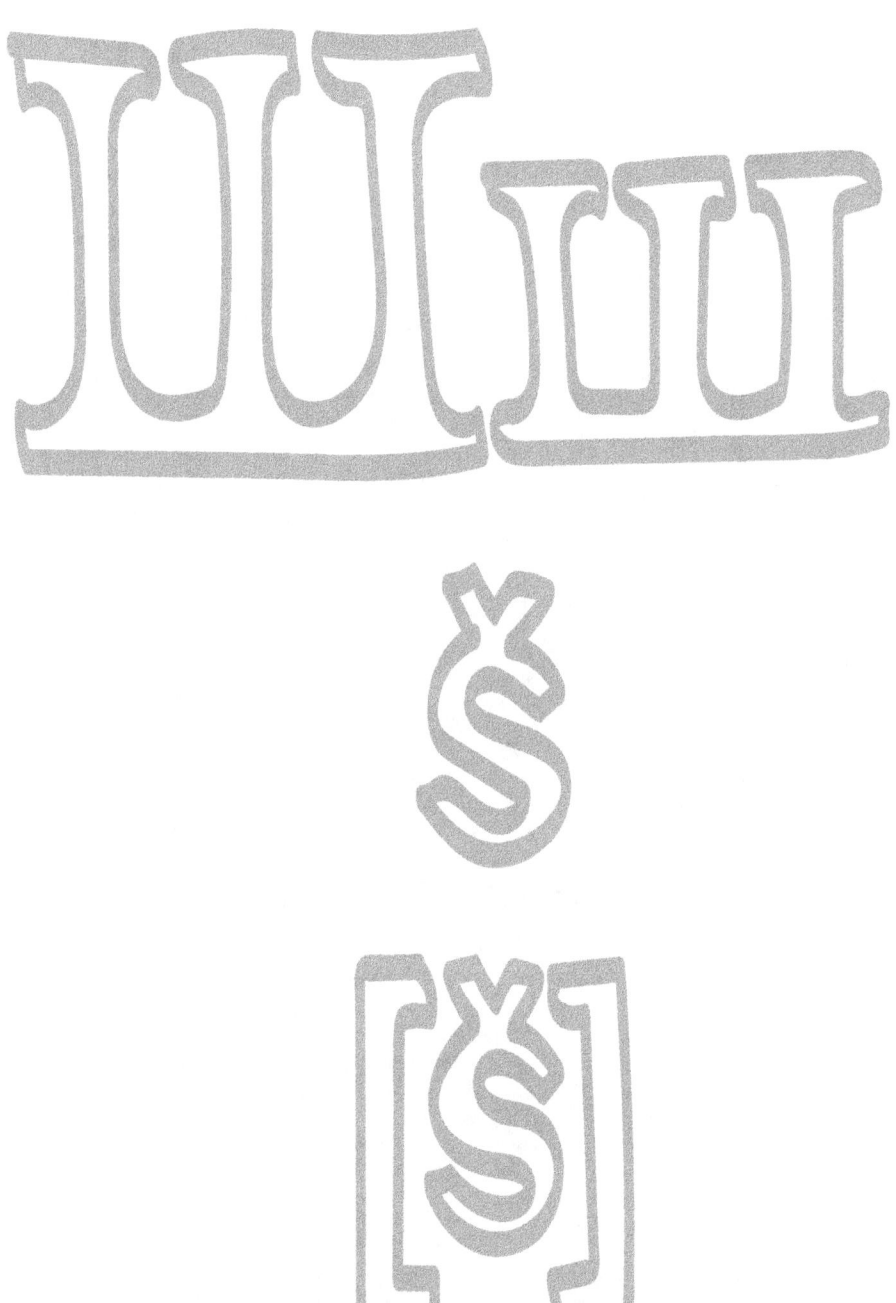

sounds like "sh" in "sharp" or "ship"

sounds like "sh" in "sheep"

Ъъ

silent

this is called the "hard sign" and acts like a "silent back vowel"

ы у [ɯ̈]

sounds like "i" in "ill"

silent

this is called the "soft sign"

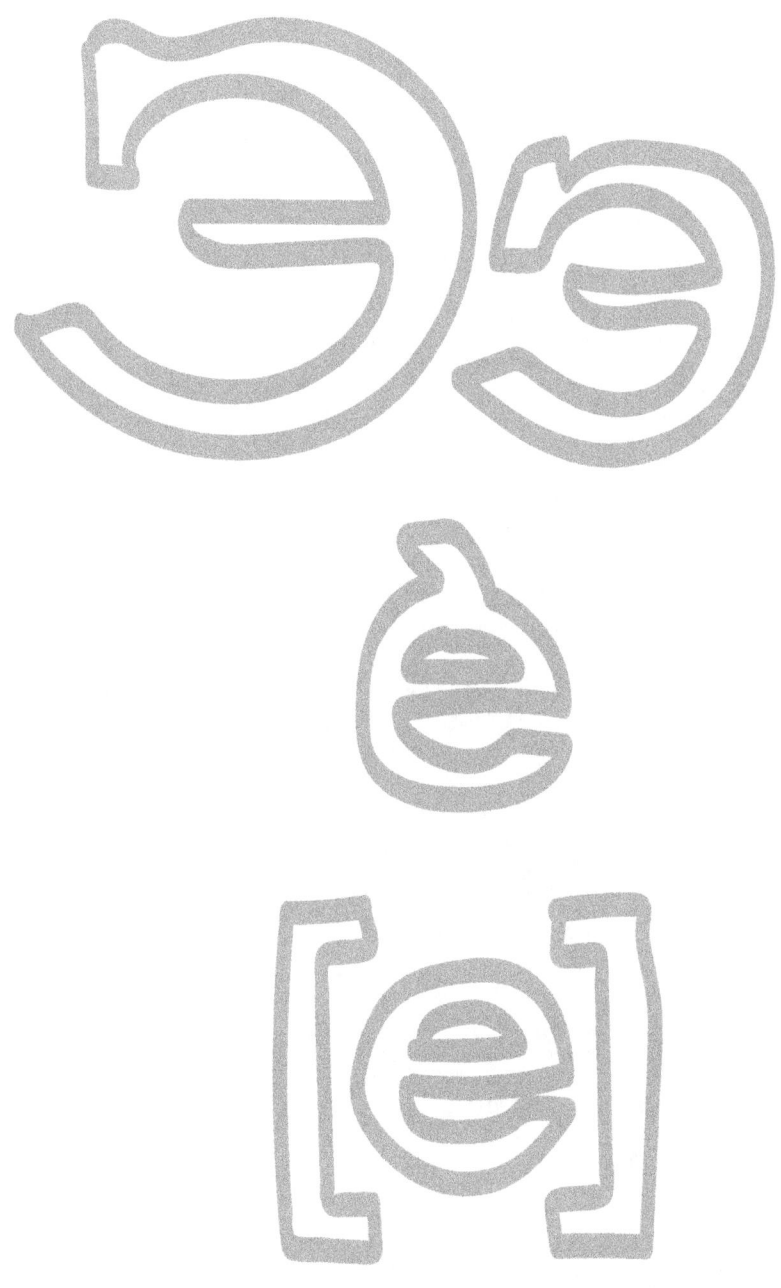

sounds like "z" in "zoo" or "zodiac"

ЮЮ ju [yu]

sounds like "you" or "use"

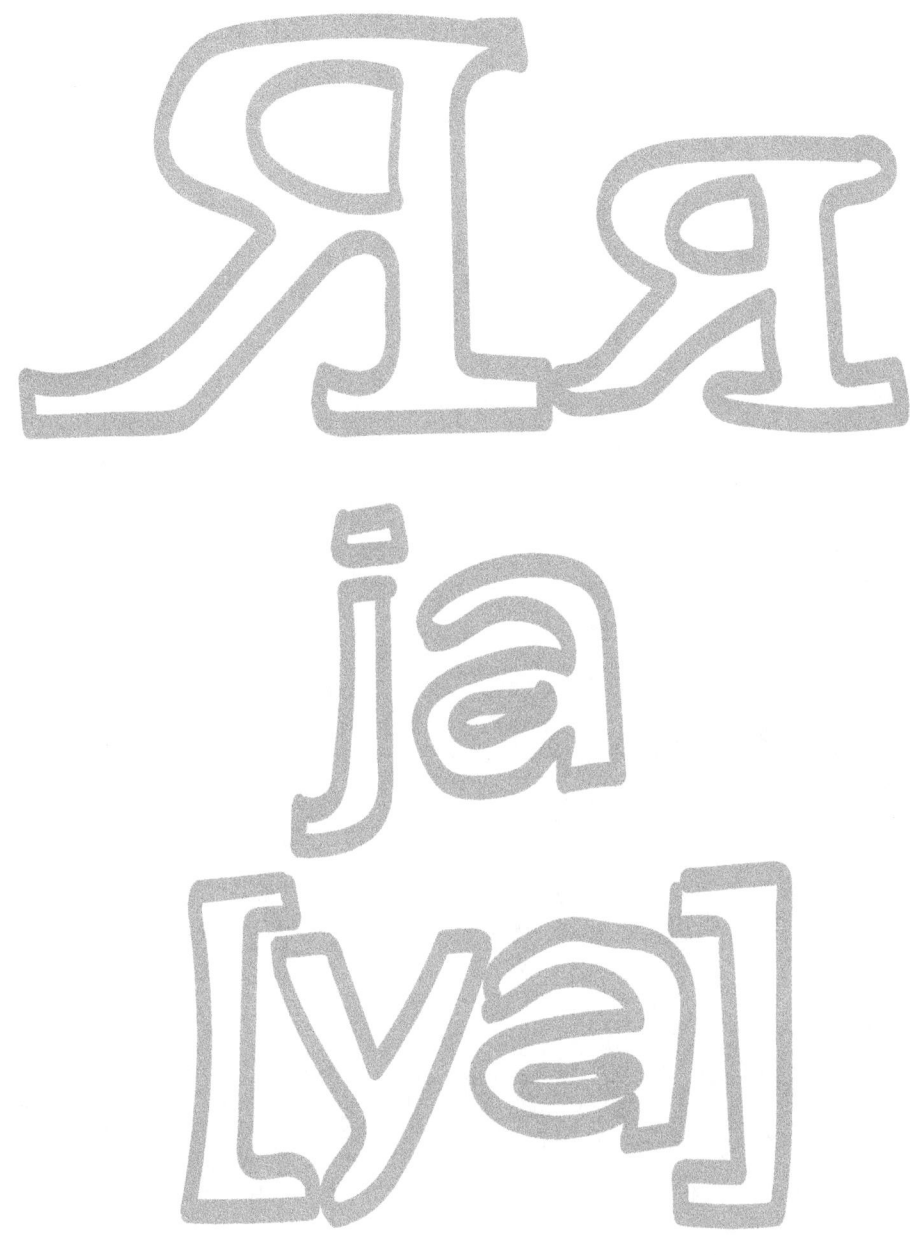

sounds like "yu" in yummy or "ya" in "yard"

www.ingramcontent.com/pod-product-compliance
Lightning Source LLC
Chambersburg PA
CBHW081349070526
44578CB00005B/784